MEASURING AND COMPARING

How Big is Big?
Comparing Plants

Vic Parker

Raintree

www.raintreepublishers.co.uk
Visit our website to find out more information about Raintree books.

To order:
☎ Phone 0845 6044371
🖷 Fax +44 (0) 1865 312263
🖳 Email myorders@raintreepublishers.co.uk

Customers from outside the UK please telephone +44 1865 312262

Raintree is an imprint of Capstone Global Library Limited, a company incorporated in England and Wales having its registered office at 7 Pilgrim Street, London, EC4V 6LB – Registered company number: 6695582

Edited by Nancy Dickmann, Rebecca Rissman, and Sian Smith
Designed by Victoria Allen
Picture research by Hannah Taylor
Original illustrations © Capstone Global Library 2011
Original illustrations by Victoria Allen
Production by Victoria Fitzgerald
Originated by Dot Gradations Ltd
Printed and bound in China by South China Printing Company Ltd

ISBN 978 0 431 00584 3
14 13 12 11 10
10 9 8 7 6 5 4 3 2 1

British Library Cataloguing in Publication Data
Parker, Victoria.
  How big is big? : comparing plants. -- (Measuring and comparing)
  1. Plant size--Juvenile literature. 2. Measurement--Juvenile literature.
  I. Title II. Series
  530.8-dc22

Acknowledgements
The author and publisher are grateful to the following for permission to reproduce copyright material: Alamy Images pp.22 (© Cody Duncan), 24 (© Fabian Gonzales Editorial); © Capstone Publishers pp.5, 7, 8, 9, 26, 27 (Karon Dubke); FLPA p.11 (John Eveson); istockphoto pp. **20 right**, **10** (© Octavio Campos Salles), **16 left** (© Kyoungil Jeon); Photolibrary pp.6 (Tetra Images), **12 left** (Garden Picture Library/ Andrew Lord), **16 right** (David M Dennis), **18** (Kalhoefer Kelly); shutterstock pp.4 (© FloridaStock), **12 right** (© Vibrant Image Studio), **20 left** (© Elena Elisseeva); www.artdirectors.co.uk p.14 (Lawrence Reemer).

Photographs used to create silhouettes: shutterstock, cactus (© Alegria), redwood (© Steven Bourelle), palm (© Viktoria), daffodil (© AlexandraStock), sunflower (© Kudryashka).

Cover photograph of a group of sequoia trees called bachelor and the three graces in Yosemite national park (2008). Image reproduced with permission of Alamy (© Astrid Harrisson).

Every effort has been made to contact copyright holders of material reproduced in this book. Any omissions will be rectified in subsequent printings if notice is given to the publisher.

Contents

Words appearing in the text in bold, like this, are explained in the glossary.

What is big?

When we use the word big, we are talking about the size of something compared to something else. For example, a cruise ship is big compared to a motorboat.

A cruise ship is longer, taller, and wider than a motorboat.

It is not always easy to work out which thing is the biggest. To decide if one thing is bigger than another, we often have to look at more than one measurement.

Is the carrot or the orange bigger? The carrot is longer but the orange is wider.

Height, length, and width

When we measure an object, we can look at its height, length, or width. The height of something is how tall it is. An object can be tall or short.

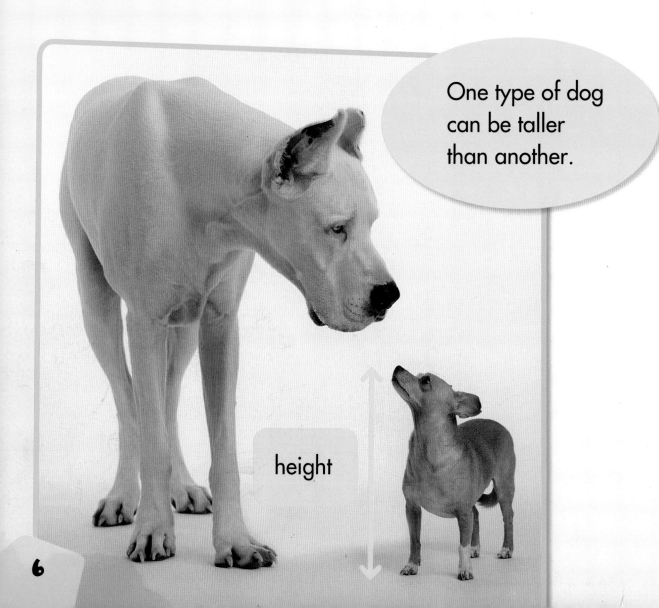

One type of dog can be taller than another.

height

The length of something is how long it is. An object can be long or short. The width of something is how far it is from side to side. An object can be wide or narrow.

An aubergine is wider than a French bean.

width

length

Measuring size

We measure something's **length**, **height**, and **width** to find out how big it is. We measure big sizes in metres (m), smaller sizes in centimetres (cm), and very small sizes in millimetres (mm).

The length of this cucumber is being measured in centimetres.

Different tools help us to measure length, height, and width. You can use a ruler, tape measure, or measuring stick.

A tape measure can measure longer things than a ruler can.

Plants

Some plants are big, while others are small. Plants need sunlight to grow. By growing tall and spreading out wide plants can get the sunlight they need, even in crowded **rainforests**.

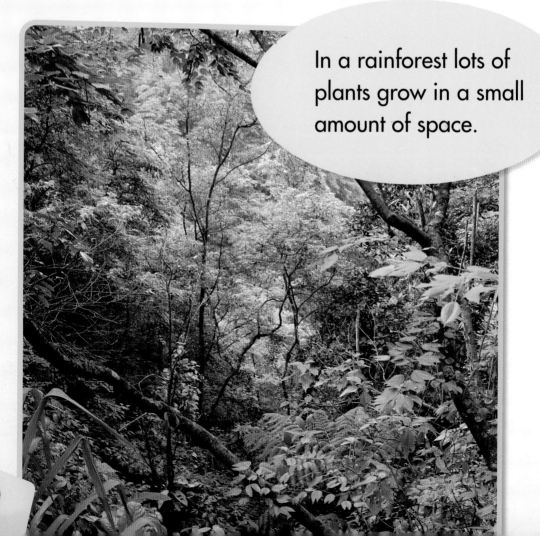

In a rainforest lots of plants grow in a small amount of space.

It takes some plants a long time to grow big. Huge oak trees grow very slowly. They don't reach their full size for about 60 years. They can live to be more than 400 years old.

An oak tree has a tall, thick trunk and long branches.

How long is a leaf?

Have you ever seen a spider plant? A spider plant's long, thin leaves can be 40 centimetres long. Spider plants come from Africa, but people from around the world have them in their homes.

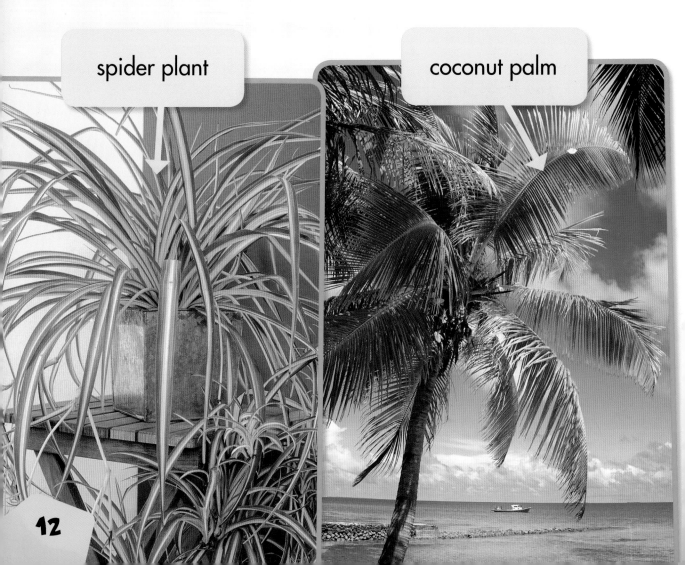

spider plant

coconut palm

A coconut palm is the tree that coconuts come from. Its leaves can be 4 metres long. It would take ten spider plant leaves to be as long as a coconut palm leaf.

Remember!
100 cm = 1 m

10 spider plant leaves

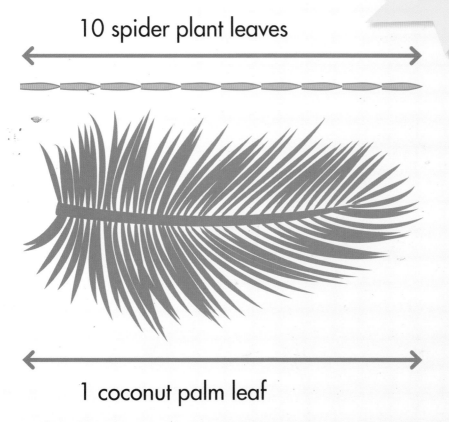

1 coconut palm leaf

What is longer than a coconut palm leaf? ➡

Palm leaves

An Amazonian bamboo palm leaf is longer than a coconut palm leaf. Amazonian bamboo palms live in warm **climates**. Their leaves are some of the longest in the plant world.

The bamboo palm tree's long leaves can be used to make hats, shoes, and rope.

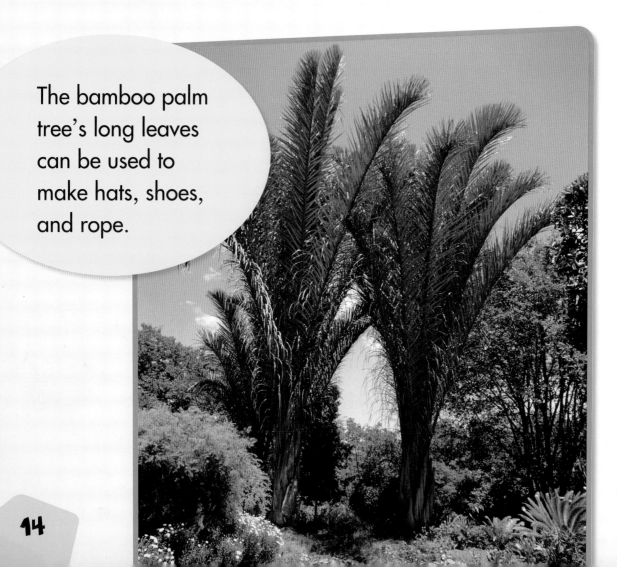

The bamboo palm's leaves can be an amazing 20 metres long! It would take five coconut palm leaves, laid end to end, to be as long as a bamboo palm leaf.

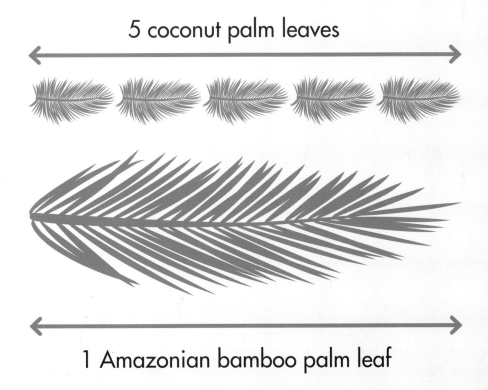

5 coconut palm leaves

1 Amazonian bamboo palm leaf

A bamboo palm leaf is long and big. What else is big? ➡

How wide is a water lily?

Water lilies grow in ponds. Their **roots** anchor them to the bottom, and their wide leaves float on the surface. The leaves of garden pond water lilies can measure 30 centimetres wide.

water lily

titan arum flower

The titan arum **flower** is the biggest flower in the world. A titan arum flower can be about 1 metre wide. This is wider than three water lilies laid side by side.

3 water lilies

1 titan arum flower

What is wider than a titan arum flower? ➡

Giant leaves

Giant Amazonian water lilies have leaves much wider than a titan arum **flower**. These plants live in waters near the River Amazon in South America.

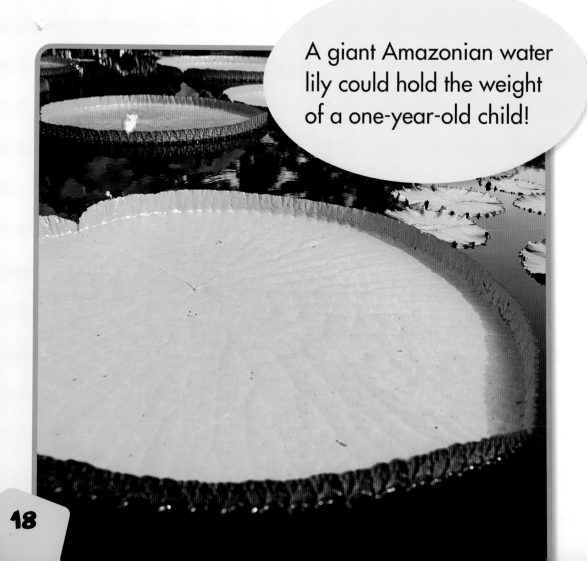

A giant Amazonian water lily could hold the weight of a one-year-old child!

A giant Amazonian water lily leaf can grow to around 2 metres wide. It would take two titan arum flowers to be as wide as this.

2 titan arum flowers

1 giant Amazonian water lily

A water lily is wide and big. What else is big? ➡

How tall is a flower?

Many plants grow tall so that they can reach above other plants and take in more sunlight. Daffodils are often seen in spring. Some daffodils are about 45 centimetres tall.

sunflower

daffodil

A sunflower is taller than a daffodil. Some types of sunflower grow to be about 3 metres tall. Six daffodils on top of each other would still be shorter than a sunflower.

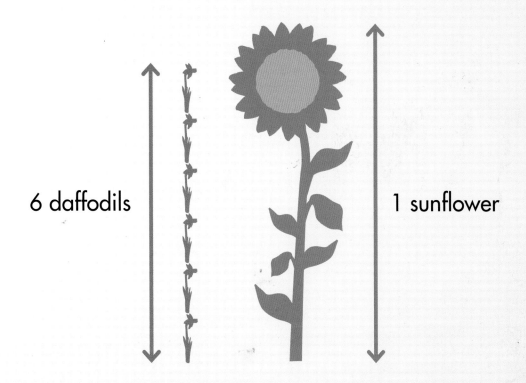

6 daffodils

1 sunflower

What is taller than a sunflower? ➡

Giant cactuses

Cactuses can be even taller than sunflowers. Cardón cactuses grow in hot, dry **deserts**. They are some of the tallest cactuses in the world.

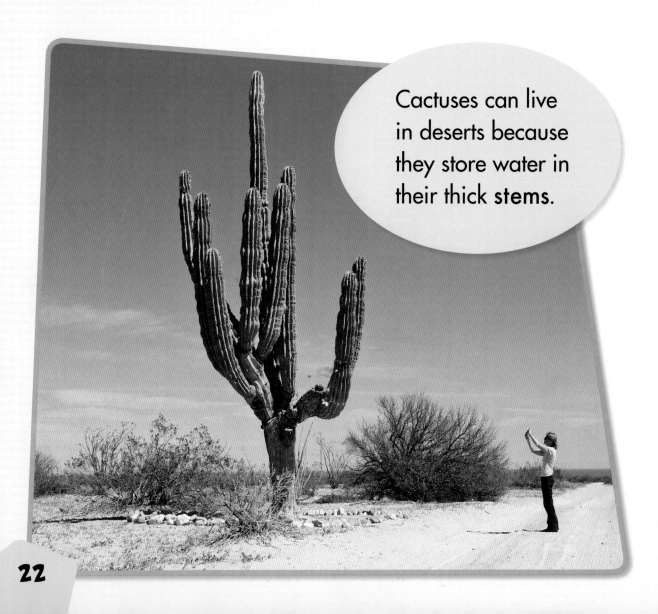

Cactuses can live in deserts because they store water in their thick **stems**.

A Cardón cactus can grow over 19 metres tall. This is even taller than six sunflowers on top of each other.

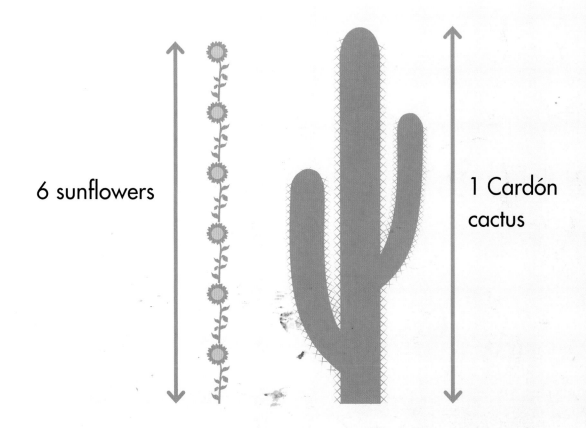

6 sunflowers

1 Cardón cactus

What is taller than a cactus? ➡

Coast redwoods

Some trees are taller than a Cardón **cactus**. Trees are tall plants with woody **stems**. Coast redwoods grow in mountain forests. They are the tallest trees in the world.

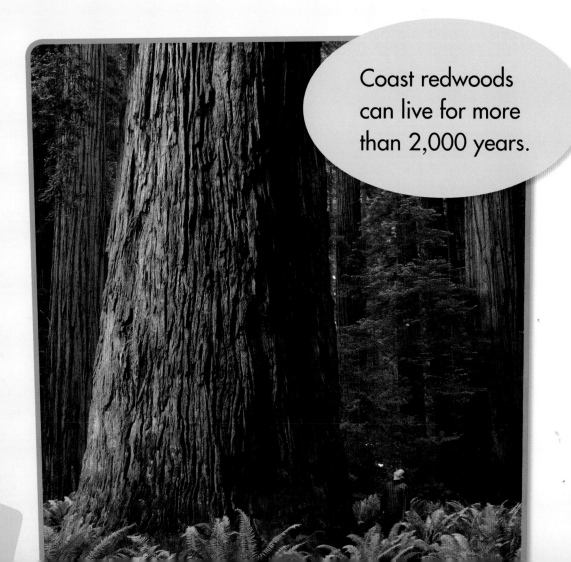

Coast redwoods can live for more than 2,000 years.

The tallest coast redwood tree is more than 115 metres tall. You would need six Cardón cactuses on top of each other to be as tall as this coast redwood.

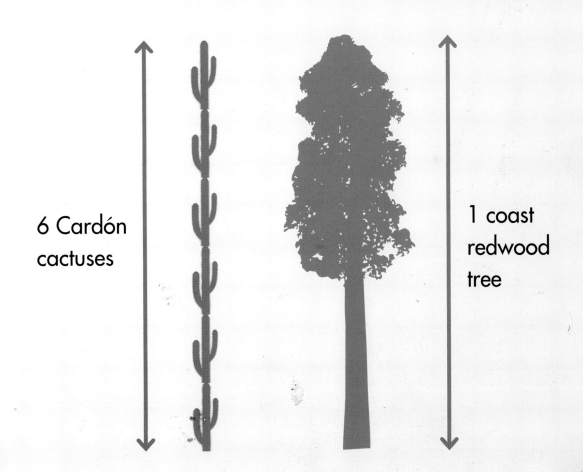

6 Cardón cactuses

1 coast redwood tree

Measuring activity

Things you will need: some leaves of different shapes and sizes, a ruler or tape measure, a pencil, and paper.

① Look carefully at your leaves. Which one do you think is the biggest?

② Measure the **length** of each leaf, and write down the results.

(3) Measure the **width** of each leaf, and write down the results.

Find out: Which leaf is the longest? Which leaf is the widest? Do you think you were right about which leaf is the biggest?

Size quiz and facts

Units for measuring height, length, and width

Very small sizes are measured in millimetres (mm).

Small sizes are measured in centimetres (cm).

Big sizes are measured in metres (m).

Quiz

1. What unit would you use to measure the **height** of a tree?

   a) millimetres b) centimetres c) metres

2. What unit would you use to measure the **width** of a sunflower seed?

   a) millimetres b) centimetres c) metres

3. What unit would you use to measure the **length** of a carrot?

   a) millimetres b) centimetres c) metres

Answers: 1 = c 2 = a 3 = b

Big plant facts

- The longest runner bean grown in Britain measured over 86 centimetres long.

- A type of seaweed called Pacific giant kelp has the longest fronds (leaf-like parts) of any plant. Each frond can grow up to 60 metres long.

- The world's widest living plant is a Montezuma cypress tree in the state of Oaxaca in Mexico. In 2005, it was measured to be more than 11 metres wide.

- The world's tallest tree is a redwood that people have named Hyperion. It grows in a national park in California, USA. It is over 115 metres high.

Glossary

cactus type of plant which mainly grows in deserts and dry places. Cactuses are often prickly.

climate the usual kind of weather in a place

desert dry area of land where it does not rain much. Not many plants will grow in deserts because the land is so dry.

flower the part of a plant that makes seeds

height how tall or high something is

length how long something is

rainforest type of forest that grows in a hot place where it often rains. Rainforests are usually crowded with lots of plants and trees which stay green all year round.

root the part of a plant that holds it in the ground. Roots bring water to the plant.

stem the part of a plant that holds it up. Stems also carry water to different parts of the plant.

width how wide something is or how much it measures from side to side

Find out more

Books

From Seed to Sunflower, Anita Ganeri (Raintree Publishers, 2006)

Plants (Investigate), Sue Barraclough (Raintree Publishers 2009)

Size and Measurement, Carol Medcalf (Collins, 2008)

Websites

www.mbgnet.net/bioplants/adapt.html
On this website you can find out about interesting plants that live in different habitats.

www.plantcultures.org
Find out about plants from all over the world by choosing them from the box on this website.

www.primaryresources.co.uk/maths/powerpoint/measuring_nearesthalfcm_mm.swf
Try measuring length and width on this website.

Index